Ribbon Topiary

As a garden art form, topiary has been around for about 2000 years. The Romans introduced this fashion throughout their empire. In Britain, topiary took off in Elizabethan times. Interest in exotically pruned gardens receded after 1750 but was revived in Victorian times.

Today, the topiary is back in favor as decorators succumb to its timeless appeal.

Looping: Shape a strip of ribbon into a circle, overlapping the ends. Adjust the size. Insert a pin, attach loop to desired surface.

Happy Harvest Canvas

Decked in gorgeous harvest hues, this canvas celebrates the season with rich color.

SIZE: 12" x 12"
MATERIALS:
12" x 12" canvas • Decorative paper • Dark Olive cardstock • Assorted ribbons (Olive Green, Cranberry, Orange, Purple, Brown) • Buttons (Metal, Colored) • Rub-on Letters • Vintage Glass glitter • *Ranger* Adirondack acrylic paints (Buttercup, Eggplant) • *ColorBox* Charcoal Cat's Eye ink • Tacky Tape
INSTRUCTIONS:
Canvas: Paint the canvas Eggplant. Let dry. • Cut decorative papers and ink the edges. Adhere to canvas.
Flowers: Cut 3 scrap cardstock circles 1¾". Use ribbons to form flowers, attaching the ends to the circle. Fill in the center with buttons. Adhere to the canvas. • Run Tacky Tape along the canvas to adhere the stems. Using 2 different ribbons, tape ribbons in streams toward the bottom right corner of the canvas, bunching, bundling or wrapping the ribbon as you go to give it a more realistic effect. • Create buds by looping one piece of ribbon 4 times. Adhere in the center with a brad and attach to the stems.
Leaves: Adhere small Green ribbon loops to the stems. Sprinkle glitter over exposed areas of tape and shake off the residue.
Finish: Adhere metal buttons to the left edge in a crooked vertical line. • Rub on the words "Happy Harvest" in the bottom left corner. • Dry brush Buttercup paint in the exposed portions of the canvas to highlight areas.

SIZE: 8½" diameter, 23" tall
MATERIALS:
5" Styrofoam ball • Wooden dowel rod • Decorative vase • Floral foam • 5 yds assorted ribbon (Cranberry, Orange, Gold, Cream, Olive Green) • 2 yds wired Orange ribbon • Straight pins • Chocolate acrylic paint • Paintbrush
INSTRUCTIONS:
Cut all ribbon 4½" long. • Wrap the ribbon into a circle and pin into the ball, covering it completely on the top and sides. • Cut dowel rod to desired length. Apply 2 coats of Chocolate paint. • Press foam into the vase. Stand the dowel rod up in the foam. Press the styrofoam ball into the dowel rod, halfway through. • Tie a large bow around the dowel rod at the base of the ball.

Friendship Card

Express your love and appreciation for your friends with this cross-hatched ribbon card.

SIZE: 5½" x 8½"

MATERIALS:
Cardstock (Dark Purple, Light Purple) • Flocked paper • Flocked letter "f" • Light Green embroidery floss • Purple flower buttons • Assorted Purple ribbons • *ColorBox* Purple Dewdrop ink

INSTRUCTIONS:

Card: Make a 5½" x 8½" card. Set aside.

Background: Trim flocked Green cardstock to 8½" x 5½". Trim flocked striped cardstock to 3½" x 5½" and adhere to the upper half of the flocked Green. Adhere ribbon in crossed pattern diagonally along the Green paper. Adhere the widest ribbon as the border along the top of the Green paper. Sew buttons at the ribbon intersections. Adhere to card.

Letter mat: Cut a Light Purple mat 2⅞" x 4¼". Ink the edges. • Cut a Dark Purple mat 3¼" x 4⅝". Adhere the flocked letter to the mats. Stitch button onto the left side of the letter. Adhere mat to card.

Adhere ribbons to card. Glue flowers in place.

Sunshine Card

Colors as bright as sunshine bring wishes for a happy day.

SIZE: 5" x 7"

MATERIALS:
Dark Purple cardstock • Decorative papers • Art wire • Assorted Yellow ribbons • Rub-on words • *ColorBox* Purple Cat's Eye ink

INSTRUCTIONS:

Card: Trim Purple cardstock to 7" x 10" and fold in half to 5" x 7". • Trim striped paper to 4¾" x 6¾". Ink the edges and adhere to the front of the card, centered, along the left fold.

Sun: Cut a 3¼" x 5" Yellow semicircle and adhere the flat side along the fold of the card. • Trim the wire to fit around the edge of the circle. Tie ribbon all along the wire. Bend in the ends of the wire so the ribbon will not slide off. Adhere the wire and ribbon along the outer edge of the circle.

Finish: Rub on the words "bliss", "carefree", "play", "delight" and "happy" to different colors in the striped paper. Cut them out. Ink the edges and adhere to the card.

1. Knot each ribbon on a wire.

2. Glue wire to the card.

If ribbons overlap, apply tape to back of ribbon. Press ribbon to page.

Silly Frame Scrapbook Page

Ribbons are an exciting substitute for papers covering this fun frame.

SIZE: 12" x 12"

MATERIALS:
12" x 12" matboard with photo cutout • Jeweled buckle • Chipboard letters • Beads • 22 assorted ribbons (Cranberry, Dark Pink, Light Pink, Lavender) • *Ranger* Adirondack paint (Eggplant, Pink) • Diamond Glaze • 1" wide Tacky Tape • Hot glue gun

INSTRUCTIONS:
Letters: Paint the letters Pink and Eggplant, alternating colors for each letter. Let dry. • Cover letters in Diamond Glaze. Sprinkle beads on top of coated letters. Cover again in Diamond Glaze. Set aside to dry.
Frame: Cover the entire surface of the mat in Tacky Tape. Adhere ribbons, including the buckle near the top left of the photo opening.
Finish: Adhere photo to the back of the frame. Adhere letters with hot glue.

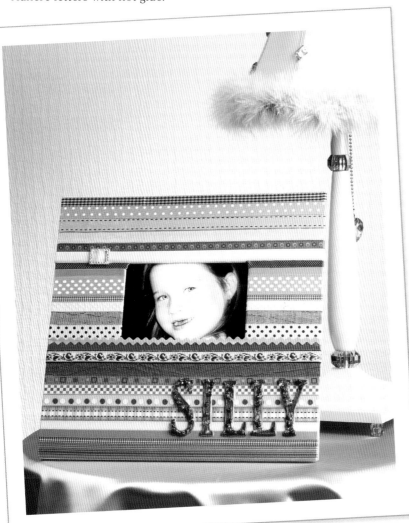

Emily Scrapbook Page

Ribbons are great for more than borders. These strips create a textural design element adding interest to the page.

SIZE: 11" x 12"

MATERIALS:
Decorative papers • Cardstock (Raspberry, White, Brown) • Assorted ribbons (Brown, Pink) • Brown buttons • Light Pink embroidery floss • *ColorBox* Cat's Eye ink (Brown, Pink) • Journaling pen (Black, White) • Glue dots

INSTRUCTIONS:
Background: Trim decorative paper to 6¾" x 12". Adhere to the left side of Brown cardstock. • Cut 3 pieces of stripe paper 2" x 4". Adhere to the right side of Brown cardstock. • Cut Raspberry cardstock 1⅛" x 12" and adhere to the page along the seam in the middle. • Cut two 3" Paisley paper circles. Cut circles in half. Ink the edge Brown. Mat one of the semicircles with Raspberry cardstock. Adhere to page. • Cut one 3½" Raspberry circle. Trim away a 3" circle from the inside, leaving a ring. Cut the ring in half. Adhere to page on the right side above the paisley semicircles.
Photo: Mat photo with White cardstock. Ink the edges with Pink. Adhere to page.
Finish: Doodle along the inside of the mats and along the bottom of the right page as pictured. Add a name and year to the bottom left corner of the photograph with Black journaling pen. • Adhere ribbons from the outer edges into the photograph, at different angles. Tie thread through each button and adhere to the ends of ribbons with glue dots.

Hi Card

Hello! Send a happy greeting just because you care.

SIZE: 6" x 6"

MATERIALS:
Two 1¼" chipboard circles • Cardstock (Orange, Light Green) • Striped paper • Sticker letters • Ribbons • Button • Embroidery floss • Metallic eyelets • *ColorBox* Chestnut Roan Cat's Eye ink

INSTRUCTIONS:

Card: Trim Light Green cardstock to 6" x 12" and fold in half to 6" x 6". Ink all edges. • Trim striped paper to 5½" x 5½" and ink the edges. Set 12 eyelets along the top and bottom of the striped square. Weave the ribbon through the eyelets and adhere the ends to the back of the paper. Adhere to the front of the card.

Embellishments: Trim Orange paper to 3" x 6". Ink the edges and adhere to card. • Adhere sticker letters "H" and "I" to the chipboard circles. Ink the edges and adhere to card.
• Cut 10 ribbons 4" long. Stack them together creating a flower. Stitch a button to the center of the flower. Adhere to card.

Stack ribbons in a circular pattern. Glue button over the center.

Love to You Card

Send a caring message with a sweet and loving card.

SIZE: 4¼" x 5½"

MATERIALS:
Cardstock (White, Rust, Golden, Sage Green) • Sheer Brown with White Dots ribbon • Rubber stamps (*Hero Arts* Love To You; *Stamps By Judith* Ladybug; *Stampabilities* Antique Linen) • Inks (*Tsukineko* Jet Black StazOn; *ColorBox* Chestnut Roan, Green) • *Lyra* Watercolor crayons

INSTRUCTIONS:
Cut Green cardstock to 5½" x 8½". Stamp the entire surface with antique linen stamp in Green ink. Fold in half to 4¼" x 5½". • Stamp ladybug image on White cardstock in Black ink. Color in the image. Trim the image to 2⅝" x 4¼". Ink the edges with Chestnut Roan. Cut a Rust mat 2⅞" x 4⅝". • Cut a Golden mat 3" x 4¾". Ink the edges in Chestnut Roan. Adhere mats to colored image.
Wrap ribbon diagonally around the bottom left and top right corners of the image, adhering on the back. Adhere the image onto the card. • Stamp "Love to You" in Green ink up the left side of the card.

Wrap corners of the paper with ribbon. Glue paper to card.

Family Ties Scrapbook Pages

Tie family sentiments together with laced ribbons on a layout joined by love.

SIZE: 12" x 12"

MATERIALS:
Decorative papers • Cardstock (Denim Blue, Light Blue, Scalloped Light Green, Sunflower, Tan, White) • Orange sheer ribbon • Plastic letters • Metallic eyelets • Jeweled brads • Black embroidery floss • *Stamps by Judith* Ladybug rubber stamp • *Lyra* Watercolor pencils • Inks (*Tsukineko* Jet Black StazOn, *ColorBox* Chestnut Roan Cat's Eye) • *Ranger* Orange Stickles

INSTRUCTIONS:
Ink the edges of 2 pieces of scalloped paper and 2 sheets of Tan background. Adhere the scalloped paper to the Tan. • Cut a 4" circle from Light Blue cardstock and adhere to the upper left corner so it overflows off the corner of the page. Trim and stitch the entire edge of the circle. Adhere decorative papers in place. Set eyelets and lace ribbon through them. • Mat photos and adhere to page. • Stamp ladybug image. Color, mat, and adhere to page. • Cut out flowers. Ink the edges, add Orange Stickles. Adhere letters and journaling in place. Attach jeweled brads.

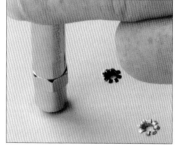

Punch holes along the edge of paper. Set eyelets in the holes.

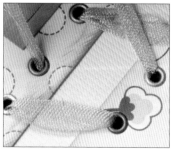
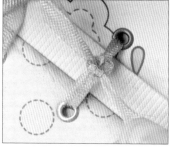

Lace a ribbon through the eyelets. Tie a knot and bow.

Burgundy Ribbon Watch

Elegant and bold, this burgundy and silver watch is a beautiful attention getter.

SIZE: 8½"

MATERIALS:
½ yd Burgundy ribbon ⅞" wide • Black embroidery floss • 2 Ribbon clasps • Watch face • Toggle clasp • Jewelry Wire • 2 crimp beads • 8 Silver beads

INSTRUCTIONS:
Thread the ribbon through the loops on either side of the watch face and measure it on your arm to determine the proper length. Cut the ribbon and attach the ribbon clasps to the ribbon ends. Sew 3 Silver beads onto both sides of the ribbon bands and 1 to each clasp. Use the wire and crimp beads to attach the toggle clasp to the ribbon clasp.

Orange and Blue Dainty Watch

Are you ready for an eclectic replacement for your watchband? Check out this ribbon and brad design with a star toggle clasp as a great finish.

SIZE: 8"

MATERIALS:
3" strips of ribbon (Orange, Light Blue) • 6 minibrads • Brown ribbon charm • Watch face • Star toggle clasp

INSTRUCTIONS:
Wrap the pieces of ribbon through the loops on the watch face and toggle clasp. Fold the ribbon and secure with brads. Attach the ribbon charm in the same manner. Attach the Blue ribbon to the opposite end of the ribbon charm, securing with brads.

Ribbon Beaded Bracelet

Do you ever wonder what to do with a few left-over beads? Make a beautiful bracelet with your favorite ribbons.

SIZE: 9"

MATERIALS:
Ribbon (12" Pink, 2 yds Black) • 16 multi-colored glass beads

INSTRUCTIONS:
Slide beads onto Black ribbon, tying a knot after each bead. When desired length is reached, tie ends together to create a bracelet. Make two bracelets from the Black ribbon and beads. Tie the two bracelets together in 3 places with Pink ribbon by making 3 bows around the 2 bracelets.

Wedding Scrapbook Page ⟶

Pleated ribbons and hearts are common motifs when decorating for a wedding. These are perfect accents for a wedding page.

SIZE: 12" x 12"

MATERIALS:
Decorative papers • Cardstock (Sparkle Striped White, Brown) • Heart die cuts • Heart frame • Assorted ribbon (Black, Denim Blue, Off-White, White, Gold) • Black journaling pen

INSTRUCTIONS:
Mat photo. Adhere to page. Adhere cut out hearts. Knot ribbons and adhere along the photo. Pleat a ribbon and adhere to bottom edge of photo. • Wrap heart frame with ribbon. Adhere paper to back of heart frame and write the wedding date. Adhere to page. • Doodle dots and swirl lines from the edges of the page to the end of each heart.

"Adorable" Buggy Card

This simple card makes an adorable announcement or invitation for a baby shower. Ribbons add a soft touch for a finished work of art.

SIZE: 4¼" x 5½"

MATERIALS:
Cardstock (Purple, Lavender, White) • Sheer Purple ribbon with White dots • *Hero Arts* rubber stamps (Script word, Baby Carriage, Sparkle Background) • *Lyra* Watercolor crayons • *Tsukineko* inks (Jet Black StazOn, Purple Brilliance, Versamark) • *Ranger* Green Stickles glitter glue

INSTRUCTIONS:
Make a 4¼" x 5½" Lavender card. Using Versamark ink and the Sparkle Background stamp, stamp the entire front surface of the card. Set aside. • Stamp Baby Carriage onto White cardstock in Black ink. Color the image. Add stickles to the leaves and grass. Let dry. • Trim and mat the image with Purple cardstock. Adhere to card. • Stamp "adorable" in Purple ink. • To attach the ribbon to the card, make small slits in the front of the card, two at each corner (one horizontal, one vertical). Feed the ribbon through the holes at each end and adhere to the back of the cardstock. Hide ribbon ends behind a piece of cardstock.

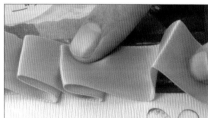

Fold pleats in the ribbon and glue to page.

Baby Invitation

Sure to please any mom to be and be the talk of the shower, these elegant vintage invitations are a snap to assemble with the added flare of ribbon.

SIZE: 4¼" x 5½"

MATERIALS:
Cardstock (Ivory, Plum, Pink, Small Scallop) • Decorative paper • Dark Purple ribbon • Vintage Glass Purple glitter • Eyelets • *Hero Arts* Baby Carriage rubber stamp • *ColorBox* inks (Velvet Cat's Eye, Dark Olive Dewdrop) • Twinkling H2O's paint • Paintbrush • Glue

INSTRUCTIONS:
Card: Make a 4¼" x 5½" Rose card. Ink all edges with Velvet. Cut a decorative paper mat 3⅞" x 5¼". Ink the edges in Velvet and adhere to the front of the card. • Using the scalloped cardstock as a template, trace the scalloped pattern along the bottom edge of the striped paper. Cut the scallops out and ink the edges. • Set 2 eyelets. Tie a ribbon bow through the eyelets. Adhere to card.

Image: Stamp baby carriage on Ivory cardstock using Dark Olive ink. Paint the inside of the carriage. Mat with Plum cardstock. Adhere to card. • Add a speck of glue to the dots on the carriage, the wheels and the handle. Sprinkle glitter over the glue and tap off the excess.

Ribbon Wreath

Create a pretty frame for an initial, name, mirror or logo with a lovely beribboned wreath.

SIZE: 15" diameter

MATERIALS:
15" Floral wreath • Blue cardstock • 4 yards each assorted ribbons (Light Blue, Dark Blue, Cranberry, White, Ice Blue) • Flowers • Jeweled brads • Straight pins • 8" monogram letter • Cornflower acrylic paint

INSTRUCTIONS:
Wreath: Tie bows all around the wreath. Tie a large loop to the top of the wreath for hanging, if desired.
Letter: Paint the monogram letter Blue. Let dry. Adhere to Blue cardstock. Run brads through the flowers and attach to the monogram letter. Trim the cardstock to fit on the back of the wreath and pin in place.

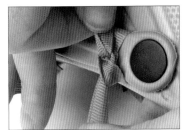

Lace ribbon through holes in the shoe. Knot ribbons around the strap.

Buttoned Up 'Crocs' Shoes

Make a statement! These Crocs are sure to get noticed.

SIZE: Women's 6-7

MATERIALS:
1 pair of Croc shoes • Assorted buttons • Assorted ribbons • Blue embroidery floss • Hot Glue

INSTRUCTIONS:
Tie floss through 45 buttons. Hot glue the buttons on top of the shoes. • Tie ribbon around the straps at the top of the shoes. • Weave ribbon through the holes at the base of the shoes.

Flip-Flops

Carefree and lighthearted, decorated flip-flops take your spirit back to those lazy summer days.

SIZE: 4" x 9"

MATERIALS:
1 pair Purple flip-flops • Multi-colored glass beads • Assorted ribbons • Simply Fabulous jewels • *Crafter's Pick* Ultimate Glue

INSTRUCTIONS:
Tie assorted ribbon around the tops of each flip-flop. String 3 beads each on 2 strands of ribbon. Tie one strand of beads on each shoe. • Adhere jewels on the base of the shoe above the toes. • Adhere rick-rack around the side of each shoe.

Blue Ribbon Planner

Make your planner as special as the events recorded within. Ribbons make it easy to add that extra special touch.

SIZE: 5½" x 8½"

MATERIALS:
Calendar Address book • Cardstock (Deep Blue, Hazard) • Decorative paper • Assorted ribbons (Orange, Green, Blue) • Jeweled brads • Rub-on letters and numbers • Flowers • Assorted vintage buttons • Embroidery floss • Tacky Tape

INSTRUCTIONS:
Book Covers: Apply Tacky Tape to the edges of the book covers and wrap the edges with Blue ribbon. • Cut papers to overlay the book covers. Ink edges and adhere to book. • Adhere a strip of Blue cardstock over the seam between the papers. • Cut polka dot paper 3¼" x 3¾". Mat in Dark Blue on the top and left sides. Add stitches around the two matted edges. Adhere to the bottom right corner. • Tie floss through the button holes and adhere the buttons to the front of the book. • Attach a jeweled brad through 2 flowers. Adhere to the top right corner. • Rub "2007" and "CALENDAR" onto the book. Rub the letters "E" and "A" on Hazard cardstock.
Page tabs: Cut 15 squares 2" x 2". Fold each square in half. Attach tabs onto the first page of every month, and at the beginning of the address book portion of the calendar. Cut 15 ribbons 2" long. Fold each ribbon in half and staple it over the tab.
Spine: Tie ribbon all over the spiral spine of book.

Baby Block Box

This adorable box is the perfect complement to the Ribbon Wreath. It's as functional as it is cute, and can be made in a matter of minutes.

SIZE: 5" x 5" x 5"

MATERIALS:
5" wooden Alphabet Box • Decorative paper • Acrylic paints (Cornflower, Bordet) • Assorted ribbon (Light Blue, Dark Blue, Cranberry) • Assorted buttons • Chipboard letters • Embroidery floss • Mod Podge • Hot glue

INSTRUCTIONS:
Prep: Paint the inside, top rim and flat sides with Bordet. Let dry.
"A" side: Paint the "A" in Bordet and the background Cornflower. Run floss through the buttons and tie. Hot glue the buttons all over the background.
"B" side: Paint the letter in Cornflower and the background Bordet. Tie floss through 5 medium to large sized buttons and hot glue along the left side. Tie a ribbon bow and hot glue in place.
"C" side: Cover side with Blue paisley paper. Mod Podge the paper onto the block. Paint the "C" with Bordet. Let dry. Adhere with hot glue. Tie 3 bows. Adhere 1 bow to a button. Glue buttons and bows to the top left side of the letter.
"D" side: Cover the side with Cranberry paper. Mod Podge paper to box. Paint chipboard "D" with Cornflower and adhere to the bottom right corner. Tie 4 bows, adhere them to the upper left with hot glue.

1. Cover the circle base with Tacky Tape.

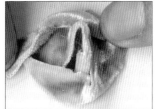

2. Beginning in the center, shape a flower.

3. Cut out cardstock backing close to flower.

Ribbon Lunch Tin

Lunch boxes are great containers for storing your favorite things like ribbons, embellishments, and craft tools.

SIZE: 4" x 7¼" x 5¼" tall

MATERIALS:
4" x 7¼" x 5¼" lunch box • Decorative papers • Rub-ons • Assorted ribbons • Alphabet mask • Assorted buttons • *ColorBox* inks (Velvet Cat's Eye, Purple Dewdrop) • Silver glitter glue • Tacky Tape

INSTRUCTIONS:
Cut papers to cover the tin. Ink the edges and adhere in place. • Adhere ribbon over seam where papers meet. Apply rub-ons. Adhere buttons. Tie ribbons around the handle. Apply glitter to center of buttons. Let dry.

Treasure Each Day Card

The one you treasure most deserves the very best card.

SIZE: 5" x 7"

MATERIALS:
Dark Spruce cardstock • Decorative papers • Rub-ons • Eyelets • Pink Velvet ribbon • White embroidery floss • *ColorBox* Chestnut Roan Cat's Eye ink • Tacky Tape

INSTRUCTIONS:
Card: Make a 5" x 7" Dark Spruce card. Ink the edges of the card.
Background: Cut 3 decorative papers 2" x 4½". Ink the edges. Arrange the strips, one on top of the other, with a small space between. Set eyelets. Rub floss across the ink. Thread and tie loops through the eyelet holes with floss. Adhere papers to the front of the card. Apply rub-on sentiment to the top left corner.
Flower: Cut a 2½" diameter circle of scrap paper. Cover the circle with Tacky Tape. Place 1 end of velvet ribbon in the middle of the Tacky Tape and gradually adhere the ribbon in a circular pattern, creating the flower. • Cut a stem and 2 leaves out of Dark Spruce cardstock and ink the edges. Adhere to the card. Adhere the flower on top of the stem.

Ribbon Bucket →

Turn an old rusty bucket into a beautiful container suitable for any room. Ribbons and beads add sparkle and texture.

SIZE: 3⅝" x 7¾" x 4½" tall

MATERIALS:
Oblong galvanized bucket • Decorative paper • Assorted ribbons (Pink, Ivory, Red, Brown, Green, Cranberry, Blue) • Large vintage button • Assorted beads • Jewelry wire • Eggplant acrylic paint • *We R Memory Keepers* Crop-A-Dile • Hot glue

INSTRUCTIONS:
Prep: Paint the bucket inside and out, including the handle. Let dry.
• Cut decorative paper into flowers and 1½" x 2" strips. Mod Podge strips onto the sides and ends of the bucket. Mod Podge flowers randomly over the bucket. Paint a gloss coating sealer of Mod Podge over the entire bucket. Allow to dry.
Beading: Slide a piece of jewelry wire through the wood handle of the bucket. The wire must be long enough to run the full length of the handle and attach at both ends. Be sure to allow enough length for bulk in the beads. String beads along both sides of the handle on the wire. Loop around the handle attachment and secure wire with a twist.
Bucket: Using the 3/16" hole punch, set your depth gauge on your Crop-A-Dile to ½". Punch holes around the top of the bucket at even spacings. Tie assorted ribbons through the holes and knot. • Adhere a ribbon around the upper edge of decorative paper. • Tie a ribbon through the button, adhere onto the bucket.

Ribbon Beaded Lamp Shade

Go from ordinary to extraordinary. Ribbons and beads bring this shade into the light with a Victorian look.

SIZE: 4¼" top diameter, 11½" bottom , 8½" tall
MATERIALS:
8½" tall lamp shade • Beads (Multi-colored jewels, Silver) • Embroidery floss • Assorted ribbons (5 Pink, 1 Brown) • Beading wire • Tacky Tape
INSTRUCTIONS:
Measure wire to go around the top and bottom of the lamp shade. When you cut the wire, leave a long tail to allow for bead bulk. • String beads along wire. When you get to the end, bend the wire over so beads will not fall off the wire. Using floss sew the beaded wire around the top rim by making a small stitch between each bead. We will attach the lower rim later. • Tape the Pink ribbon around the top of the lamp shade. Skip down 1" and attach a thinner Pink ribbon around the lamp shade. • Tie twist-knots of ribbon on the next layer. Attach each knotted ribbon at the seams. We will cover the seam later. • Skip down 1" and adhere the same ribbon you used to make the first stripe. • Tie bows and attach one in each section of the shade, near the bottom. • Tape strips of ribbon vertically along the dividing rods of the lamp, creating knots at the top and bottom. • Attach the bottom string of beads as you did the top string.

My Stuff Journal

This book is so lovely, it begs to be opened. "My Stuff" is a beautiful gift for a loved one or for yourself.

SIZE: 8" x 10½"

MATERIALS:
Hard back notebook • Green cardstock • Decorative paper • Assorted Ribbon (Brown, Pink, Cranberry, Light Green) • Rub-ons • Flowers • Embroidery floss • Chipboard letters • *ColorBox* Chestnut Roan Cat's Eye ink • *Ranger* Lavender Stickles • *We R Memory Keepers* Crop-A-Dile hole punch
INSTRUCTIONS:
Cover: Cut 2 decorative papers to cover the front and back. Ink the edges. Adhere 1 of each paper to both covers. Cut a ½" wide strip of Green cardstock to fit vertically over the 2 papers. Ink the edges and adhere. • Cut a 5" paper circle and a 5½" Green cardstock mat. Adhere circle to mat. Position circle on book cover with part of the circle hanging off the edge. Trim away overhang. Use floss to stitch the circle to the mat. Adhere to the front and back covers of the book. • Use rub-on letters to make the word "Stuff" in the bottom center of the notebook. • Adhere a string of Prima flowers along the edge of the Green strip. Put a dot of stickles in the center of each flower. • Ink the chipboard letters to create the word "MY", and adhere to the circle. • Randomly apply rub-ons to decorate the cover. • Punch 2 holes in the upper right corner of the book and attach ribbon through holes.
Page Tabs: Cut 10 Green cardstock 2" squares. Fold each square in half. Cut 10 pieces of ribbon 2" long. • Apply a small bit of adhesive onto each inner side of the folded squares. Place each square along the edge of the desired page, sandwiching the page inside the fold. • Fold a ribbon in half, staple over the squares to create tab.
Spine: Tie ribbons to spiral spine of the book.

Rustic Christmas Ball Ornament

Whether hung from a tree, dangled in a wreath, or displayed in a bowl of other decorative balls, this ornament adds a natural rustic look to any vintage setting.

SIZE: 7" diameter

MATERIALS:

Stick ball ornament • Assorted ribbon (Pink, Ivory, Red, Brown, Cranberry) • Assorted vintage buttons

INSTRUCTIONS:

Tie knots all over the surface of this ball and then cut the ribbon tails to the desired length. Tie decorative buttons onto the ball randomly. Tie a long loop on top for hanging.

Ribbon Tree

Bring in the holidays with style with this stunning tree made entirely of ribbon! Holiday visitors will "Ooh" and "Ahh" over this amazing creation. You'll never be prouder to have decorated for the Christmas season.

SIZE: 10" diameter base, 29" tall

MATERIALS:

24" tall Styrofoam cone • Paper mache Star wand • 5 yards each of 25 assorted ribbons (Red, White, Pink, Purple, Light Green)
• Straight pins with ball heads • "E" beads • Diamond Glaze
• Diamond Dust • Acrylic paint

INSTRUCTIONS:

Star: Paint the star and part of the wand handle. Cover the star in Diamond Glaze and Diamond Dust. Pierce the handle of the wand into the top of the styrofoam cone and push the star into place.

Ribbon: Cut all ribbon into 4½" strips. Form each piece into a loop. Stick a straight pin through the ends of the ribbon. The tree will look better if all the pieces of ribbon are going roughly the same direction. Begin pinning the ribbon on the tree starting at the bottom, and work your way up to the top. To add sparkle to the thinner ribbons, thread a bead onto the ribbon before pinning.

When finished, examine the tree and fill in any loose places or holes, fluffing the ribbon as you go.

Christmas Star Ornament

Add a pinch of patriotic cheer to the spirit of Christmas with the Star ornament. It's the perfect finish for any package.

SIZE: 5" x 5" x ½" deep

MATERIALS:

Star paper mache ornament • Assorted ribbon (Pink, Red, Light Purple and Dark Purple) • White embroidery floss • Assorted buttons (Blue, Dark Purple, Light Purple, Red) • Vintage Glass glitter (Gold, Pink) • *Ranger* Wild Plum Adirondack acrylic paint • Diamond Glaze • ½" wide Tacky Tape

INSTRUCTIONS:

Paint the star. Let dry. • Run floss through the buttons, tying in the back. Set aside. • Draw a wavy line from the top to the bottom of the star. Tape ribbons in horizontal stripes. • Tape ribbon around the side to cover the ends of the ribbon stripes. Adhere buttons • Pour Diamond Glaze over the remaining half of the star. Sprinkle with glitter and let dry.

Christmas Button Flower Ornament

This pretty button flower makes the perfect base for a package tag. After the package is opened, display the ornament proudly on your tree as a colorful work of holiday art.

SIZE: 6½" diameter

MATERIALS:

Paper mache disc 3⅝" diameter • Assorted ribbon (Pink, Red, Light Purple, Dark Purple) • 40 assorted buttons • White embroidery floss • *Ranger* Wild Plum Adirondack acrylic paint • Tacky Tape

INSTRUCTIONS:

Paint the disc. Let dry. • Cut 24 pieces of ribbon 4" long. Fold each ribbon in half and adhere to the disc. • Run floss through buttons, tying in the back. Adhere buttons in place.

MAGIC

Celebrating a wedding is one of the most memorable events in our lives. Help the happy couple remember the magic with this stunning centerpiece, embellished with ribbon, Diamond Dust and beads.

SIZE: 8" x 27"

MATERIALS:

Paper mache letters (M, A, G, I, C) • Decorative paper • Assorted Ribbon (Black, White, Lavender, Violet) • Bead heart • Ring • "4-Ever" License plate • Tag Embellishments • *Ranger* Eggplant Adirondack acrylic paint • Paintbrush • Diamond Dust • Mod Podge • Pop dots

INSTRUCTIONS:

Prep: Paint letters. Trace the letters onto decorative paper and cut out. Mod Podge the paper onto the letters.

Run a dry brush with paint on it over the letters in various spots. Paint over the letters, front, sides, and back with Mod Podge. While the Mod Podge is still wet, sprinkle Diamond Dust over the entire surface of each letter. Dust off excess Diamond Dust.

Letters: Knot ribbons. Adhere embellishments as desired.

Stacked Gift Boxes

Beautiful boxes hold the promise of delights within. Use these as a decoration or give them to family and friends.

SIZE: 4¼" and 7¼" diameters

MATERIALS:
Round paper mache boxes (4¼" and 7¼" diameter) • Decorative paper • 50" Green sheer wired ribbon • Pink ribbon (1 yd ⅝" wide, ½ yd ⅛" wide) • *ColorBox* Pink Cat's Eye ink • Olive Green acrylic paint • Paintbrush • Mod Podge • Tacky Tape

INSTRUCTIONS:
Paint both boxes and lids, inside and out. Let dry. • Cut paper to cover the sides of each box. Ink the edges. Mod Podge paper to box. Let dry. • Adhere paper to top of each lid. Adhere ribbon around the edge of each lid.• Create a large bow with Green wired ribbon. Stack boxes with the bow on top.

Measure the box. Adhere ribbon to box.

'SARAH' Wall Letters

Ribbon accents and pretty papers beautify wood letters for a wall decoration that is too lovely for words.

SIZE: 6½" x 25"

MATERIALS:
6½" tall wooden letters • Decorative paper • Assorted ribbon (Light Blue, Dark Blue) • Ribbon charms • *ColorBox* Chestnut Roan Cat's Eye ink • Acrylic paint • Mod Podge • Sandpaper

INSTRUCTIONS:
Paint letters White. Let dry. • Trace letters on decorative paper and cut out. Mod Podge paper on top of letters. Let dry. • Sand and ink the edges of the paper. • Embellish with ribbon and charms.

This is a close-up photo of the completed flower.

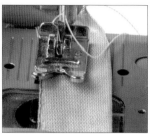

1. Sew a Running stitch down the center of the ribbon by hand or with a sewing machine.

2. Pull the threads to gather up ribbon to the shape of a flower.

3. Sew each ribbon flower to the bag.

4. Glue a gem, bead or button to flower center.

Brown Eyes

A circle of buttons complement the ribbons in this fun layout.

SIZE: 12" x 12"

MATERIALS:

Cardstock (Dark Blue, Denim Blue, White, Cajun) • Decorative paper • Chipboard letters • Embroidery floss • Silver ribbon clasp • Vintage buttons • Sticker Verse • 1 yd Brown ribbon ¾" wide • 2 Black brads • *ColorBox* Charcoal Cat's Eye ink • Journaling pens (Black, White) • Corner punch • Paper piercer

INSTRUCTIONS:

Page 1: Background: Cut 8 decorative papers 2½" x 6". Cut across the diagonals to make 16 triangles. Ink the edges. Piece 6 triangles together, points facing inward toward the center of the paper, in the upper right corner and the lower left corner of the first page. Adhere the triangles as you go.

Photo: Mat the photo with Dark Blue. Wrap the bottom with a Brown ribbon. Run the ribbon through either side of the Silver clasp and adhere the ends with brads. Adhere photo to page. • Adhere buttons in a circle around photo. Place a soft mat underneath your page. Using a paper piercer, make holes in the paper through each hole in all the buttons. Stitch thread through the holes.

Tag: Adhere the verse sticker to Denim cardstock and trim. Mat on Dark Blue cardstock, creating a tag. Staple a piece of ribbon to the end of the tag and adhere in place. Adhere 2 pre-threaded buttons to the end of the tag.

Page 2: Background: Adhere triangles in place. Adhere 11" of ribbon. • Cut a 5" x 11" rectangle of Denim paper. Ink the edges and adhere to the page. Adhere the "e" and write "yes".

Photo and Journaling: Mat photo and journaling box in Dark Blue. Adhere to page. Adhere photo corners in place. • Mat the "b" with Light Blue. Adhere to page. Write "rown". • Sew buttons to page.

Striped Bag with Ribbon

Everyone will wonder where you bought such a unique tote bag! You can proudly tell them, "I made it myself".

SIZE: 13" x 16½"

MATERIALS:
2 place mats 14" x 18" • Assorted ribbons • Assorted buttons • 1 yd ribbon with beaded dangles • Ribbon flowers

INSTRUCTIONS:
Sew ribbon to one side of each place mat in vertical strips, completely covering the place mat. Sew beaded ribbon along the length of one place mat. Just above the beaded ribbon, sew another line of coordinating ribbon. Sew a line of assorted buttons above the row of ribbon. Sew ribbon flowers in place.
• Cut handles to desired length and stitch on the back of the place mats.
• With right sides together, sew sides and bottom seam. Turn right side out. Sew buttons at the base of the handles.

White Tote with Ribbons

Pretty enough to take everywhere, this easy tote is a snap to make.

SIZE: 13½" x 18"

MATERIALS:
2 place mats 15" x 20" • Ribbons (1 yd Black grosgrain 1" wide and 1 yd Gold ⅞" wide for handles, 2 yds Brown satin 1" wide, 1 yd Green sheer 1" wide, ½ yd Pink metallic ½" wide) • Assorted buttons • Flowers

INSTRUCTIONS:
Sew 2 pieces of Brown ribbon across each place mat, 1" apart. • Sew the Gold ribbon to the Black grosgrain. Cut the ribbon in half. Sew a handle to the back of each place mat. • With right sides together, sew the sides and bottom seam. Turn the bag right-side out. • Sew bows to the ends of the handles. Sew buttons, ribbon, and flowers in place.

 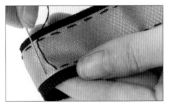

Measure the handles. Center a ribbon on each handle and sew in place by hand or sewing machine.

Button Box

The colors of the 70's come alive in a delightful button box. This sweet box makes the perfect storage container, or gift box.

SIZE:
6½" diameter
5" tall

MATERIALS:
Scalloped round paper mache box • Assorted ribbons • Assorted buttons • Embroidery floss • Chocolate acrylic paint • Strong hole punch • Tacky Tape • Hot glue gun

INSTRUCTIONS:
Paint the box and lid Chocolate, inside and out with 2 coats. Let dry.
• Run Tacky Tape around the base of the box, ¾ of the way up. Adhere the ribbon around the box in stripes.
• Tie floss through each button. Attach a row of buttons around the top of the stripes, allowing room to close the lid. • Punch holes around the sides of the lid. Weave ribbon through the holes and tie a bow in front. • Adhere buttons, covering the top of the lid.
• Tie 6 small bows and glue them at even increments along the outer edge of the top of the lid.